Free and Low-cost

Online

Promotional Techniques

for

Indie and Self-publishers

of Kindle and POD

Paperbacks

by

Matt Lashley

Disclaimer

Although the author and publisher have made every effort to ensure that the information in this book was correct at press time, the author and publisher do not assume and hereby disclaim any liability to any party for any loss, damage, or disruption caused by errors or omissions, whether such errors or omissions result from negligence, accident, or any other cause.

Table of Contents

Introduction

When you write a book and self-publish, you are not just a writer but also a publisher. This means you are a business owner, and there are things you need to do that are not related to writing. This is an uncomfortable part of self-publishing for many writers, and the truth is that many are not cut out to do this type of work. But do it you must. The most important aspect of self-publishing is marketing, and a successful self-publisher can easily spend as much time doing promotional work as writing a book.

Of course, there are many ways to market a book, and most of them cost money. The chances are you don't have a lot of money to spend on advertising, but there are many things you can do to promote your book that cost little or nothing, other than your time. And this type of promotion is where you want to start. You will learn more about your readers, what attracts them to your book, and how best to reach them. And these lessons won't be expensive, the way many paid advertising campaigns can be.

The marketing of a book starts with the book itself. Choosing a topic then writing a quality book is half the job in marketing. Because without demand, it is difficult to near impossible to sell something. However, it is not absolutely impossible because good marketing can create demand, but you want to avoid being in this position with a book, especially non-fiction.

The number of books you write will have a direct bearing on the sales of all of the books. I'm not talking about total sales, that is obvious, but the sales of each individual book. Slow selling titles will show an increase in sales, as other books in your catalog have high sales. This is true as long as you have quality books on topics that currently sell. Over time, most books in the world of non-fiction will continue to sell. Sometimes they must be revised to bring them current, but they will still sell. The type of non-fiction books that no longer sell and will never sell are those that have become obsolete and cannot be brought up to date, but these titles are rare. One example, would be a best-selling book on repairing VCRs. A best-selling book on this subject over time, experienced a drop in sales until today, at best, there is only a rare sale to an electronic hobbyist.

This book is written for the writer who has self-published his or her book, and how to go about promoting your book with a small, promotional budget. Its main focus is on print-on-demand books via Amazon's Kindle Direct Publishing and digital books via Amazon's Kindle and other eBook platforms.

Book Cover

Long ago, the publishing industry discovered that simply changing covers on their paperback books could increase sales dramatically. You may already have a cover, but you can always change the cover. And if you haven't made your cover yet, you should take care to make something that is appealing.

If you don't have a lot of money to spend for a nice cover, you can use the free cover creator on Amazon. You can also use a low-cost cover creation website such as MyeCoverMaker.com. They allow you to use their tools for free, but if you make something you like, it will cost you a small fee to download your design. You may want to look at the website called Fiverr. There are good graphic artists who can make you a good cover at a low price.

Identify Your Audience

If you're a writer that is willing to write non-fiction books on a wide range of subjects or fiction books in one or more genres, you should first do research into where the demand for books lie. You can, of course, write what you like, but that doesn't mean it will sell. There is a business to writing. Perhaps not as much on the writing side, but as a publisher, it's all business. So before you begin to write a book, you need to put your publishers' hat on.

It is important in marketing to know who your customers are. Although many write their book and then go in search of an audience, you should have a general idea who your readers are before you start writing. Once you leave the world of Amazon, knowing your audience is critical to advertising. You should first find your readers, and then determine the best way to reach them with your advertising message and of course, write a good ad. But on Amazon, readers are already there. Amazon is the largest selling platform for books – hard copy or digital books. You need only identify the subset of readers that you're looking for. Most of the marketing is limited to finding your readers through optimizing your book for Amazon's search engine, but you can also advertise on Amazon. I will discuss this later in the book.

Maximizing Your Books for Search Results

Search result ranking on the Amazon website is one of the most powerful ways to sell a book. Unfortunately, there is not a lot you can do to maximize your search results placement without resorting to something that goes against Amazon's terms of service. Although the exact algorithm used by Amazon to determine search result placement is unknown, it is clear that there are several obvious factors. The following are the most important, and a few observations on how they relate to a small publisher.

The number of reviews and quality of reviews are important

I will write about this separately. Suffice to say, reviews are important enough that Amazon gives them special attention. There has been a lot of abuse in the past by gaming the system with fake reviews. Amazon has clamped down hard. Although reviews are important in search results, they are not the only factor.

How many times the book's page listing has been visited

This is a function of many aspects of marketing. Naturally, part of it will be the ranking is search results, and this will be a function of your marketing effort. However, the number of backlinks there are to a book has a big influence on search results. Backlinks are simply the links that exist on websites, blogs, forums, social media platforms or other internet sites. Amazon loves it when people find your book outside the Amazon platform. There are many ways to generate links to your book to the Amazon catalog page, and I will discuss them throughout this book when it is applicable to the topic.

How many copies a book has sold

For this reason, you need to focus on selling your books. Your placement in search engines will rise accordingly. When a book begins to sell well, it is easier to find in search engines, so it will sell even better. Sales create more sales.

The title of your book

Your title is critical with non-fiction books. If your title is keyword rich, readers will likely find it in Amazon search, as long as the topic is not saturated with titles. In that case, you will need other marketing techniques besides your title, but the title of your book is a powerful search factor. For fiction books, it can be tricky. Depending upon the genre, it may be possible to sneak in a keyword or two that relates to the genre you are writing in, but usually you will need to pay attention to other factors to help with search engine placement.

Your title is something you need to put a lot of thought into prior to publication. Once you have an ISBN assigned for a paperback book, you will not be able to change the title. With a Kindle book, you can simply delete your book and publish it again with a different title. So if you haven't created a paperback yet, you can revisit your title to make sure it's what you want before attempting a paperback. Once your paperback is in the Amazon catalog, it will not be deleted. Although, you can simply create a new title with a new ISBN, then ignore your first book title. It will remain in the Amazon catalog, and slowly slip into oblivion.

Category

You can choose the category you want your book listed in, as you begin the process of publishing on Amazon. Although listing in small niche categories can mean a high ranking in sales for that category, this is a process that occurs before you begin writing. After you have written your book, the only thing you can do is choose the category that closely matches your material. But if you are doing research for a book, you can look for these smaller categories, and then write for that category. You really need to be a good generalist writer to do this, but there is something to be said for marketing research before you write. But after you have written you still need to find the best categories for your book.

Keywords

Amazon allows you to enter up to seven keywords for your book, and you need to use all seven keywords. They don't need to be single words; they can be a small phrase. These keywords take on greater importance for a work of fiction because it is difficult to use keywords in your title. And although these keywords are not the most important element for high placement in search results, they play a part. So make sure you take the time to select the best words or phrases for your book. Keep in mind that if you realize later that you should have included a word or phrase you left out, you can always go back and make changes.

Book Description

A good book description that has keywords related to the content of your book will be picked up by Amazon's search. However, you should make sure that the keywords flow naturally with the description, and you are not spamming the keywords. Only use them when needed. Your book description is important enough in marketing your book that I have given it a separate section.

Book Description

Although a book description can help in search results, its primary purpose is to sell your book after a prospective customer lands on the catalog page. There are many ways this can happen. A person may find your book from an outside link, but however they arrived, you want to entice them to make a purchase.

Amazon allows you to use up to 4000 characters, and you should try to use as much as possible. But don't attempt to write ad copy simply to use up all the space that is allowed. Make sure everything you write is an important part of selling the book

Do not write a wall of text. Break up your description into small, easy-to-read paragraphs. For non-fiction, they need to understand the importance of reading your book while a reader of fiction should feel a sense of excitement towards the entertainment that awaits him or her.

You should also use HTML when possible

HTML stands for Hypertext Markup Language. This is the language that your browser sees, then interprets for you, so it displays the way a programmer wants you to see it. Although Amazon allows only a limited amount of HTML, what is available can be helpful to your book description. If you don't know anything about HTML, you can learn the basics at:

https://www.w3schools.com/html/default.asp

It's not that difficult. Here is a link to the HTML allowed by Amazon.

https://kdp.amazon.com/en_US/help/topic/G201189630

The bold and italic symbols are ones that I use the most. Both are easy to use. Simply begin the text with the symbol without the slash and end the symbol with the slash. For example, to make a sentence bold, you use the symbol to begin, and then finish with the symbol. For italics, you begin with <i> and finish the sentence with </i>.

Other HTML I like to use are the <u></u> symbols for underline and <h4></h4>, <h5></h5> and <h6></h6> to increase the font size.

And of course, <br> for line breaks.

Pricing

When people hear the word marketing, they often think of advertising or perhaps promotion in general. But advertising is only one part of marketing. One of the key components of marketing is pricing. Marketing your book means having the right price for your book. If your price is too high, you may not get many sales or none at all. If your book is priced too low, then you are leaving money on the table. You want to get the maximum amount of profit you can from each sale of your book. The bad news is that there is no way you can know what this number is, at least not in the beginning. Add to that, the perfect price point will be different for each book you publish. So what is the best way to go about pricing your book?

If it's too high, you'll lose sales. If it's too low, you're not making as much money as you could be making. But here's where books are easier to price than other products, at least for a print-on-demand and/or electronic publisher. All you need to be concerned with is not starting your price too high. If the book is priced too high, you will not know whether your sales are low because of price or because there is no demand for your book. Look at comparable books for guidance on where to start your pricing, but try to start your price below the comparable books.

It is better to start low. If your book doesn't sell, you will know that it isn't the price.
At that point you can attempt to use various promotional methods. However, if you price the book low and it begins to sell without much promotion, you can begin to slowly increase the price until you hit a resistance point. You can do this with print-on-demand books because you are not likely to sell more than one copy per customer, and you can change the book's price in a matter of hours. The same holds true with digital books.

In book publishing, it's usually one and done. Future customers will not likely be aware of the price increases because they have never bought your book before, and most likely, never saw it listed in a catalog. The only repeat customers you are likely to see is for another, similar book you have published.

Author Central

Amazon allows an author to have an author page to provide a great deal of information about their books and themselves. Most of the features are easy to use, and Amazon provides easy-to-follow instructions. You can get more information here:

https://authorcentral.amazon.com/

You can only do this for a single author, so if you write under two different names, you will only be able to use one of them. For fiction writers, this may be disappointing. You may be a good writer of two genres that do not have much crossover readership, for example horror and romance, but Amazon will only allow one. You will have to decide which author name is better suited for your author page.

Book Reviews

Everybody wants to have a lot of five-star reviews on Amazon, but the truth is that reviews are hard to come by, both good and bad. Most people don't leave reviews after reading a book. This is especially true with a Kindle or other digital books, but paperbacks are usually not reviewed much either. There is a temptation to buy reviews. There are plenty of people who will give you a review for money on many of Fiverr and other such places. DO NOT DO THIS! It is against Amazon's Terms of Service, and you can lose your account. Another technique is to swap reviews with other writers and publishers. There are various ways to do this, but all of them are against Amazon's TOS as well, so you should never engage in this because you may find your account terminated.

I know it can get depressing when you see so many books with a lot of reviews and wonder where they get them, but many of them are fake. When you see a newly released book with 30 or 40 reviews and all of them are four and five-star ratings, with most of them five stars, almost always, these are fake reviews. And when Amazon gets around to it, these reviews will be taken down, and these people will inevitably lose their accounts. Keep promoting your books, and the reviews will come.

Reviews are a bit overrated, though. On one hand, reviews are clearly a part of the Amazon algorithm for search results placement. But every scammer knows this, and Amazon is always watching for those gaming their system. It is not worth the risk. And besides, high search result placement is more than reviews, and search results is only one part of promoting your books.

Of course, you may think that good reviews will help to sell books, and there is no doubt there is some truth to this, but it is not cut and dry. Perhaps it is more true with certain types of books. I sell mostly non-fiction, and the star ratings are a mixed bag. The worst selling book in my publishing catalog is one of the best reviewed books. On the other hand, I had a best-selling book for three years straight that never received a single review. When someone finally reviewed the book, it received four stars.

With fiction books, reviews are more important because people are less likely to take a chance on a book without knowing what others are saying about the book. Non-fiction, on the other hand, can have no reviews, but if the topic is of interest to the reader, they may go ahead and buy a copy.

You can ask for a review, but don't ask for a good review. At the end of the book you can request a review, and even provide a link. You probably won't get a lot of reviews by doing this, but you may get a few. But be prepared for both good and bad reviews.

So what does all of this mean? Don't spend too much time fussing over reviews. Take a comprehensive approach to promoting your books. Follow the paths that are most productive for you, but let the reviews come organically. Attempting to take a shortcut with fake reviews is not worth the risk. Real authors and publishers are in this business for the long haul.

Expanding Your Format Offerings and Distribution

Other eBook Platforms

Assuming you have Kindle book, you should be aware that there are other important sites that can provide a lot of sales, if your book is popular. Apple and Barnes & Noble are two of the biggest. The problem is that it takes time to format your book and upload to all of these sites. There are, however, two eBook services you can use where you upload a single file, then they will list it on various sites for you. You can call them eBook distributors, if you will. One is Smashwords, and the other is Draft2Digital. Smashwords has been around for a long time, but I have never used them before. I do know they have requirements for formatting that you need to learn. With Draft2Digital, you can use the same file you used for your Kindle book. It is very easy. Draft2Digital is a younger company than Smashwords, but they have made a good reputation for themselves quickly. Part of this is because they do make it easy to use their service.

Both companies take a commission on top of the fee charged by the venue that is listing your book, but this is standard procedure for any type of distributor. They are acting as a middleman, so it will be more expensive. But I have found their service worth a slightly higher commission. It is a huge time saver to only upload a single file. In addition, in order to format for iTunes, the Apple platform, you need a Mac. Since I use a PC, I would need someone to do this for me, and that would cost money. But Draft2Digital takes care of the formatting for you. Just remember not to have any links to Amazon in your eBook or Apple will reject your book. If that happens, all you need to do is remove the links. Apparently, Apple and Amazon do not get along.

Keep in mind that if you are enrolled in Kindle Select, you will not be allowed to list your book on other digital sites. But this rule only applies to each book, so you can experiment with where your books make the most money. In Kindle Select, you will earn money from Amazon's KENP program, where you will earn money for page reads along with your sales. On other digital platforms, you will earn money for sales but sacrifice the money from KENP. I have found that non-fiction doesn't lend itself well to KENP, and since I publish almost all non-fiction, I have most of my books listed across multiple platforms via Draft2Digital.

One last thing to consider. If you made your book cover with Amazon's free cover creator software, you will not be able to use this cover on other platforms. You will need to make a new one. There is low-cost software online such as MyeCoverMaker.com, or you can explore low-cost options on Fiverr.

Expanded Distribution

If you have a paperback book through KDP this is simple to do. It's just a matter of checking the box for expanded distribution when you are publishing your book. It is a part of the pricing section. Before you agree to this, you should understand two things. The first is that your royalties will be much less than when a paperback is sold on the Amazon platform. You are paid 40 percent instead of the usual 60 percent of the sale. Of course, this is before printing costs, so the actual net difference between an Amazon sale and expanded distribution will vary. Another issue to be aware of is the time lag for expanded distribution sales to begin to show up in your sales reports. It can take several weeks. These numbers will not show up throughout the month either, but only at the end of the month in one large dump of sales numbers.

Large Print Editions

This is not something that is as big of a factor with non-fiction, but it can be important for those who are writing and publishing fiction. Large Print books are important for those who have low vision, but still find reading enjoyable. I should point out that as a type 2 diabetic with diabetic retinopathy, I have low vision in both eyes. For this reason, I made a Large Print edition of a book I wrote on diabetes, and this sold almost as much as my smaller font size edition. But this was a special type of non-fiction book that had a built-in audience for a larger font size.

In the publishing world, Large Print editions are often produced by a different company than the regular editions. An author will sell the rights to a Large Print publisher. However, as an indie or self-publisher, you can publish your own Large Print title. Naturally, you will only be doing this for paperbacks because electronic readers can change font size with the tap of a finger.

Here is a quick run down on how I create a Large Print paperback. It should be noted that I follow the guidelines stated by the Low Vision Community authored by the Council of Citizens with Low Vision International: An Affiliate of the American Council of the Blind. Their website can be found at https://www.acb.org/large-print-guidelines.

Amazon also has guidelines, but they seem to be slightly more liberal than those set forth by the organization mentioned above.

The two biggest differences between one of my regular books and a Large Print edition is the font size and font style. Obviously, you need a larger font size. I use a minimum of an 18 point font. Since my normal minimum is 12 point, I simply increase all 12 point to 18 point and then increase any font greater than 12 by six points. There are a few different font styles recommended by the Council of Citizens with Low Vision International. As you might imagine, they are very plain and easy to read. I choose to use Arial for all of my Large Print Editions.

Here is the procedure I follow:

Starting with the file you used for your paperback edition, change everything to Arial font. (remember to save the file under a new name)

Change 12 point font size to 18 point font size
Add 6 points to everything above 12
You will need a new ISBN for your Large Print Edition. If you are an indie or self-publisher, you are likely using a free one assigned by Amazon. If so, you need to start the process of publishing and getting an ISBN. I also like to place the ISBN in the same location as my other books, the copyright page. The one difference is that I like to print in all capital letters and in a large font – LARGE PRINT

EDITION.

LARGE PRINT EDITION
ISBN: xxxx

I also like to add the words LARGE PRINT Edition to the back cover of the book, and increase the font size of the book description that I have written. This may not seem important, but if you have your paperback in expanded distribution, including libraries, it will be important. People will actually be picking up your book from a rack or off a shelf to read the back for the description.

Although I used the same book description in the Amazon catalog page for the Large Print edition as I do for the regular edition, I do like to add the following line at the top of the description:

This book is a LARGE PRINT format paperback using an 18 pt. Arial font.

I also like to bold this sentence.
Since I use HTML in my descriptions, it looks like this:

This book is a LARGE PRINT format paperback using an 18 pt. Arial font.

Other than the added sentence above, the rest of the description is cut and paste from my regular paperback. The same is true with the keywords.

You should remember to check the "large print" box that is listed on the description page. By doing this, Amazon will note in the title area of the catalog page that the book is a Large Print edition.

Here is the Large Print Edition Checklist

1) Change everything to Arial font

2) Change 12 point font size to 18 point font size

3) Add 6 points to everything above 18

4) Change back cover to read LARGE PRINT (all caps)
Increase font size of back cover description, if possible, otherwise edit down.

5) Add new ISBN to inside of book and the words: LARGE PRINT EDITION

6) Change book description for Amazon catalog to read:

This book is a LARGE PRINT format paperback using an 18 pt. Arial font.

Place this at the beginning of the description, and remember to use HTML tags.

7) Check the large print box.

Audio Editions

An audiobook can mean additional revenue for a book, especially one that is beginning to catch on. Amazon offers self-publishers the opportunity to have an audiobook through their program known as the Audiobook Creation Exchange (ACX). They go so far as to allow you to select someone to read your book, but these professional voice actors come at a price. However, with limited funds, you can read your own book. You only need a computer and some recording software, as well as the ability to edit your audio tracks. Of course, you will need a place that is quiet. But if you have the time, this doesn't need to cost a lot of money. And besides, people seem to be fond of hearing the author's voice when they listen to audiobooks. For more information, I recommend reading all the information that is available at Amazon. You can find it here:

Foreign Language Translations

This isn't as big of a sales boost with non-fiction. Unless you're writing on a topic of study that people want to learn about in countries all over the world, it is probably a waste of time. Some travel books may have potential, but it is in the area of fiction that foreign language translation holds the greatest potential for sales. Of course, you should have a fan base in the English language first before you attempt to do this. Translating a book can be expensive, but if you're bilingual, you may want to consider doing the first language translation yourself.

Using Kindle Select for Promotion

Once you have enrolled your book in Kindle Select, you are committed to 90 days of exclusive listing on Amazon. In exchange for this, you are allowed either five days to offer your book for free, or you can do a countdown promotion. This latter option allows you to advertise your book at a reduced price for a short period of time. You're not obligated to choose a promotion, the other benefit is that you will earn money for page reads for those who have a subscription. Although the payment is below a half cent per page read, for some authors, this can be a significant amount of money. However, in this section I will be writing about using the five days of free downloads for any Amazon customer that is interested.

Giving away books may seem counter-intuitive for selling books. After all, books are not a commodity like a food item. You can give away a free sample of a cookie, and if people like them, they may come back for more. This is obviously not true with books, but there are a few exceptions. For this reason, you need to give away a certain type of book. One that you don't plan on selling.

There are two types of books that you can use. A book that is not a big seller or creating a small publication specifically for a free digital promotion. Keep in mind, that you are only attempting to give away an eBook. Even when a book doesn't sell well in digital formats, it may begin to sell better in paperback, after a Kindle promotion. I have had books that sold well in paperback but not Kindle. In fact, my paperbacks sell better than all of my eBook listings combined. People still buy paperbacks. For that matter, many of my books are set up so that a customer who buys the paperbacks, can have the Kindle version for free. This is called Matchbook on Amazon, and I regard it as a customer service rather than a source of revenue.

Ideally, you can use a free book promotion with a publication that is related to one of your other books in your publisher's catalog; however, this is usually a good idea for non-fiction. With fiction, you may want to consider giving away the first book in a series, or perhaps a collection of short stories in the same genre of the other books. Giving away fiction is an effort to build up a fan base. You also need to get people's emails and build up a list of people interested in your books, so you can send out announcements when you have a new publication. The more popular you are with readers, the larger your initial sales will be upon release of the next novel. The most popular writers in every field of fiction have fans who anxiously anticipate the writer's next novel.

Non-fiction is different. With a few exceptions, such as political commentary, non-fiction authors are selling information. So when you sell a book, the reader may be satisfied and may not need any more information. The idea is to write or publish a mix of books on the same subject, so a reader who likes one book may be interested in related books. Off the top of my head, one example might be a book about growing certain types of flowers in your backyard. You may also publish other books that relate to gardening, such as growing berries. By giving away one book, you may be able to increase sales of other books.

A word of caution: you need to use a book that simply doesn't sell well, at least in the digital format. By running a Kindle Select with free download days, you may be sacrificing sales for that book, so you want the sacrifice to be as little as possible. It should also be a book that doesn't sell well in digital format on other sites such as Apple or Nook Press. This is because you won't be allowed by Amazon to sell on any other digital platform if you choose to enroll in Kindle Select.

Whether fiction of non-fiction, giving away books for free can be used to generate reviews, which in turn, can drive up sales. You will need to ask for a review at the end of the book. But although you can ask the reader for a review, you can't ask for good review. So be forewarned, you may not like all of the reviews you get. To make matters worse, few people will bother giving your book a review after reading it. There is a tendency for people who dislike a book to have more motivation to leave a review rather than those who loved it. You will also find that there is a certain number of downloads you will need to generate a single review. Part of this is due to most people not leaving reviews, but there is also the issue of people downloading a book for free that they never get around to reading. People love free things, even if they have only a passing interest in it.

Permanently Free/PermaFree eBooks

You can make a book permanently free, then promote your freebie however you want. Draft2Digital allows you to select a book to offer free, so all places you choose to list your book through Draft2Digital will list it free. There are exceptions. The most notable is Amazon. Amazon is tricky because $0.99 is the lowest price you can list a book, but here is how you get around that. Amazon has a policy of requiring the price of a book to be at least the same or lower on Amazon than the price it is listed on a competitor's site. After listing your book for free elsewhere and giving Draft2Digital enough time to list it as such (this is usually 2 to 4 days), you can email Amazon to let them know the book is free on other sites. Once they confirm this, they will drop the price from $0.99 to free.

I have done this in the past with Amazon, and to be honest, I have had problems. The first is getting them to do it. So if you email and nothing happens, you need to email a second time. Give them a week to take care of the issue. I have also had a book become permafree, then go back to $0.99. So you need to monitor your free books on

Amazon to make sure they do not mysteriously revert to $0.99. If you decide to try this, make sure you have a listing of all books that you publish in the back of the book. You should also list a website, blog, or a social media platform to get the most out of a free promotional book.

If you decide to use Smashwords, you will not have any of the problems getting Amazon to list your book for free. Although I have not used Smashwords for a permafree book, I know they have a similar free listing option as Draft2Digital, but unlike Draft2Digital, they have the ability to list it on Amazon for free.

Fiverr Promotion

Fiverr is a platform that allows people to offer a wide variety of services starting at five dollars. These services are called gigs, and can offer great value to an entrepreneur. As a publisher, I have used services for promoting books, and the design of book covers and have found Fiverr gigs to be helpful to my company's success.

Most people offering promotional services on Fiverr will only accept business from those promoting a free Kindle book or one for 99 cents. However, the majority of these promotions will be for Kindle books that are free. This means a book that is running a free download promotion for Kindle Select or one that is permafree.

Choosing a gig for your promotion
Obviously, you want someone who has good reviews while keeping in mind that everyone will get some bad reviews. Other than this, you should look for those with at least 20 ratings. Don't take a chance with someone who is just starting out. You should also pay attention to the location the freelancer is working out of. This can affect the success of the gig. Certain books may not be popular in the

freelancer's country. For example, if they are in Europe and the people they will be promoting your book to are all European, this may not be fruitful for a book that is only of interest to Americans. So the lesson here is to have an idea who your audience is. For fiction, it may not be as important, but if you write in English, you want to market your fiction to English-speaking people first. English language readers outside of English-speaking countries do exist, but the numbers are small.

Many freelancers will offer add-on services or different tiers of service. You should avoid doing this until the basic five dollar gig is successful.

Also keep in mind that a freelancer may offer a service that is successful for one book but not another. I have had this happen several times. So if you have more than one book, and they are different types of books, it is possible for one book to be promoted successfully and another unsuccessfully, using the same Fiverr freelancer.

Keep in mind that combining Fiverr with Kindle Select free downloads has its limitations. The problem is that you are using it to promote your promotion on Kindle – in other words, a promotion for a promotion. It sounds strange, but as long as your goals are met, then it will be worth it. However, it's difficult to succeed with free downloads.

Increasing the Number of Books You Offer

As a writer of books, you are engaged in a business, but unlike many businesses, you will not be dependent upon repeat business unless you write more than one book. Readers do read a book more than once, but they seldom buy it more than once. You can build up your readership and make money off the purchase of new titles from the same readers.

When marketing your books, you must think like a publisher and nurture your catalog. This is true whether you are the author of all of the books in your catalog or have published one or more other authors. If you only have one book that you wrote, you must still think as a publisher. You have only one book in your catalog, this means you need more. More books will help sell other titles in the catalog.

One of the most powerful ways to promote your books is to have a lot of them. Naturally, you don't want to publish poor quality books, but the more quality books you have, the more you will sell. But I am not talking about the total amount you will sell, that is obvious. I am talking about the average sales per book. This is a phenomenon that I have noticed as a publisher. I would, and still do, breakdown the sales for each book title by month. Looking back at previous sales, it becomes clear that the more books I publish, the higher the average monthly sales are per title. Of course, not every title sells as well as others, but on average, I can see most titles going higher in average sales.

In addition to publishing more books, you need to make sure that there is a list with a description of each book in your catalog. I prefer to place this in the back of the book because placing it in the middle or at the beginning will be an irritant to readers.

Promotional posts

You can promote your books on the internet simply by writing posts on various platforms. The trick is getting your name along with an occasionally, subtle plug for a book. For non-fiction authors, you want to demonstrate knowledge, so readers will be attracted to what you have published. Fiction authors may find discussion groups, relating to the genre of the books they have written, fruitful. The following are just a few ideas of where you may be able to post.

Facebook

Of course, you need to be a member to post on these groups. Although most groups are open to new members, occasionally an administrator will close the group temporarily because of the rapid growth of the membership. A group will also shut down, or the administrator will archive it, so no new posts are possible. Although Facebook groups will come and go over time, there are many that have been around for a long time. If you can find one or more that relates to what you write about, it could be beneficial to participate.

Reddit

I'll admit, I like Reddit a lot more than Facebook. Granted, it is a different type of site. Whereas Facebook is geared towards the socializing online, Reddit is more of an elaborate forum, and I have always enjoyed forums. The thing about Reddit though, is it takes some getting used to, so you need to spend some time clicking and reading about the site. Once you learn to use it, the site is easy to navigate.

Reddit, like Facebook, also has groups, but they are known as subreddits. There are so many it takes time to find ones that fit your books. You also need to find those with frequent postings.

Like Facebook, you will find groups that are dedicated to the listings of free Kindle downloads. They can be valuable when you are creating a couple of days of free downloads and are looking to maximize the number of people aware of it. I have found subreddits for free Kindle books to be more fruitful than those on Facebook. But you need to pick the right subreddits. The ones with the most members are naturally the place to start.

Join forums

Forums are discussion boards and are a great way to achieve links to your website or blog. In most forums you are allowed to have a signature, and in this signature you can put a link to your website.

Two important things to keep in mind:

1. Make sure it is a forum you are interested in. You must be able to make comments that are pertinent to the forum topic.

2. No Spam. And when I say this, I am talking about any post which has as its sole objective, promoting your book or website. That your website is listed as a signature in your posting, should be clear even to the most casual of readers but is secondary to the comments made on the topic under discussion.

AMS Ads

There is an old saying, "It pays to advertise." But on the other hand, you can easily spend more money than you generate with book sales. For this reason, I have left out any discussion about search engine ads on platforms such as Google, Facebook or any other ads on the internet. AMS ads are the one exception. These are advertisements that are listed solely on Amazon, and this is where the lion's share of books are sold online or offline, and if you're careful, it is not expensive.

AMS stands for Amazon Marketing Services, and as it relates to promotion, it means pay-per-click advertising. Although similar to other pay-per-click advertising programs, Amazon is where most of the books on the internet are sold, and outside of Google, it has the largest search engine on the internet. As a book publisher, this is the place you want to be.

I'm not going to go into detail about how to open your account and set up an ad for your book because Amazon already does a good job of that in their help pages, so it would be a waste of time. However, I will give you some understanding about the basic way it works, along with a few tips.

How it works

The keyword brings up the ad, but the ad is what produces clicks. The ad consists of not only the text but also the cover and the ratings. The star ratings listed in the ad are the least important. If you are getting clicks but no sales, this is the fault of your book page. Getting someone to click on any ad, Amazon or elsewhere on the internet, is half the battle. Once the prospective customer arrives at the catalog page for your book, it is up to you to convert this to a sale. Some of this is related to reading your reviews, but there is nothing you can do about reviews unless you want to put your account in jeopardy. Your description, however, can be improved. If your getting clicks but no sales, go back and look at your description. Chances are there is a lot of room for improvement.

Although I spoke of pricing in an earlier section, it is with your AMS ads that you will get the best information on the price of your book. If you are not getting clicks at all, it is possible that your book is priced too high.

Keywords

If you have a non-fiction book that has a keyword rich title, you don't have to be concerned with choosing the right keywords. Simply choose automatic targeting, and Amazon's algorithm will do the rest. The real issue is with fiction books. Your title may have few, if any, keywords in it. You will need to choose words to use for targeting. You can experiment with as many words or phrases that you can come up with. You will need to monitor your words every week or so to see which ones are getting the most clicks. You can drop the words or phrases that aren't working and add others that you have thought of. Initially, I would recommend downloading Amazon's spreadsheet template. It's easy to use. Just enter your keywords and upload the file.

Bids and budgets

Start your first ad with a low bid. For me, this is usually five cents, unless I have a feel for the type of book I'm advertising. This is important because if you don't get many clicks, you can always increase the bid price. However, if you start high and get clicks, you may be spending too much without realizing it. If someone clicks on your ad when it's 50 cents, how do you know they would not have clicked on it for less money? You can easily spend too much on each click when you start high. Yes, it's true that you can limit the daily spending amount of your ad. But if you set this to a figure that is low like a dollar, but you have your click number at 50 cents, you have a price per click at 50% of your daily budget. This is much too high to generate enough information to analyze.

You can click on your ad in the dashboard to make adjustments. You can add or delete keywords, raise or lower the bid amount, and you can adjust the maximum daily amount spent on the ad.

Keeping records

You need to keep records of what you are doing. The AMS dashboard is terrible for ad analysis. Decide ahead of time what you want to track. Although the dashboard will track impressions, clicks and sales, it is done for each ad. If, for example, you want to track the results of two different texts, you will need to have two different ads. This becomes problematic because running two or more ads will result in each ad competing with the other ad. So test ads using the classic A/B technique is simply not possible. What I like to do is keep one ad, record the impressions, clicks and sales, then make the changes to the ad. I can then tell how well the changes are performing.

More than one book format

Another thing to think about is having more than one format for your books. I have always found that my AMS ads are more successful if I have both Kindle and paperback editions. I think it's because many people still like buying and reading paper books versus digital books. I know I do. That's not to say that I never read digital books. I do. It's just that I prefer hard copy books. If someone were interested in your book, and they click on the ad, only to find a digital edition but no paperback, you could lose a sale. Having said that, if you don't have a paperback book, then you won't notice any difference. On a side note, you may want to experiment with having a separate ad for a Kindle format and a paperback. They can be the same ad. In my experience, they don't compete with each other because they have separate ASIN in the Amazon catalog. Sometimes having an ad for each format can increase sales.

Understanding ACOS

Average Cost of Selling is one of the columns of information on your AMS dashboard. Although this information is valuable, the way it is displayed is deceptive. They list ACOS as a percentage of your sales, but it doesn't take into account the expense of selling your book. Of course, there can be a variety of expenses associated with selling a book, but even as a gross cost of sales, the percentage in your dashboard is deceptive because it doesn't factor in the download cost for a Kindle or the printing cost of a paperback.

If you only have a Kindle book with a minimum size, your break even point will be right at 70 percent, as long as the book isn't a large file due to photos and graphics. The 70 percent figure is the royalty earned for your Kindle book. With paperbacks, there is the printing cost, and this will almost always be more significant than the download cost of a Kindle. You will need to check your sales reports for exact information. But it is important to know where your break even point is for ACOS, so you will know if running your ad is worth the cost.

Also, a big issue is that at the time of this writing, they don't break down your ACOS by paperback and Kindle. If you are running an ad, it tells you the number of sales you had, but it doesn't say which format the sale was made in. This is frustrating, but there is nothing you can do about it.

Final advice

The most important thing to remember when you first start using AMS ads is to go slow and be cautious. You will learn what works best for your book and what to expect from AMS ads as a marketing tool.

Website or Blog

If you are a writer, you really should have a website or a blog. If you don't know the difference, relax. Practically speaking, they are the same. However, a blog is a specialized version of a website that is frequently updated and allows for reader comments. Of course, if you turn off the reader comments function of a blog and don't update it often, I suppose it is more of a website. But websites offer more than the latest blog entries. There are longer articles and other types of information such as forums, but the truth is, for your purpose as a publisher, either type of web presence works fine.

It doesn't cost anything to get started with a blog. In fact, you can get a free blog. One popular free blog can be obtained from Google's Blogger.com. It doesn't cost you anything but your time to set up the blog. It is easy to learn, and you can create a blog in as little as an hour.

You can explore a free blog from Google at their free blog site.

https://www.blogger.com

Another option is WordPress.com. This is similar to Google's Blogger. You get a free blog and you get a domain name that is hosted by WordPress. There is nothing to buy.

One of the benefits of a free blog is, just that, it's free. But if you are willing to spend a few extra dollars, you can get your own domain name. Then, for a few dollars a month, you can have a company host your blog. Of course, you will need to have a blog first, and the easiest way is to start with the most popular blogging software on the internet – WordPress. It is free to download, and you can create your own blog. But there is a learning curve to using WordPress.

What you can do is find a company that has what is called managed WordPress. For a fee, they will host your blog and provide WordPress software that allows you to easily create your blog and update it. Many of these companies will also provide domain registration. One example of this is GoDaddy. You can register your domain and pay an annual fee, usually around $15. You can also get a managed WordPress site for around $10 a month. There are other companies that offer this service too, but this is a popular company and one that I am familiar with. (Full disclosure, I am not making any money by mentioning GoDaddy).

Using your own domain name and paying for web hosting gives you the advantage of control over your site. The free sites always have the option of censoring you or removing your blog if they choose.

Although a blog can serve to advertise your books, there is still the problem of driving traffic to your blog. The best way to do this is with quality content. Search engines are looking for quality backlinks to your site, and the frequency of fresh content being uploaded. It takes time for your blog to get noticed on the web, but it is just as difficult for one of your books to get noticed in the ocean of books listed on Amazon. But if you write articles and blog entries that are interesting, and ones that will relate to your books, people will naturally be interested in your books. You will want to link your book titles with cover images to Amazon. Equally important is to mention your blog in your books, so traffic will be generated in that direction as well. Your blog will help your books sell, and your books will help your blog sell titles as well.

Building and Using an Email List

An email list can be a powerful marketing tool. But the trick is to have a list of people who are interested in your books. It is possible to buy these lists, but they can be expensive, and their effectiveness is questionable. The best lists are those that you have built yourself. Although this takes time, it doesn't cost much money to accomplish.

If you want to build an email list, you need to have your own website. This means getting a domain name registered and finding a company to host your site. You can still use WordPress, but you should have your own domain name and not use the free WordPress website/blogs at wordpress.com.

You will need an automated software program that allows visitors to your site to sign up to your email list for notifications of new book releases or other important news. The one I would recommend is Mailchimp. There are two reasons for this. One, I have used this program before, and two, it is free. Well, at least it is free up to a couple thousand subscribers. But if you can build up a list of 2,000 subscribers, you are doing great as an author.

Mailchimp allows you to create a landing page that people will see when they arrive at your site. It is a simple box that allows your visitor to give a name and an email to be added to your list. Undoubtedly, you have seen these on the internet and may have signed up at one or more websites yourself. Landing pages are fairly simple to integrate with your website, but if you are using WordPress, they have a plugin. This is what I have used in the past.

There are many advantages to having an email list. You can keep in touch with your fans. All you need to do is compose a newsletter, and with a couple of clicks, you can send it out to everyone on the list. A program like Mailchimp will also allow those receiving your email to opt out. This means you will have a quality list of readers who are interested in your books.

When you are ready to publish a new book, you will be able to inform your readers when the date of its release will be and how to purchase it. A percentage of those on your list will be ready to buy your new book immediately, and many of them are likely to leave reviews. These initial sales and reviews can build up momentum, then Amazon will likely promote it for a period of time after that. They will show it high in search results and include it in emails that they send to their customers, based on their browsing habits. If sales are high enough, you may break into the bestseller category, and your sales will go even higher.

Social Media

I'm skeptical of the value of social media in marketing. Having said that, there are a few writers that have had success with it. The problem with social media is no different from having a website or blog. No one is going to stumble upon your website. You need to drive traffic to your site. The same is true with social media. People don't stumble upon your Facebook page or an Instagram page. You have to promote your page in order to get views and likes.

If you want to use social media, I would recommend that you choose one platform and focus your energy there. Facebook is a good choice because of the many options available to a user. You can use it like a website or a blog. You can even start your own group, but it should be a topic that relates to your writing. Of course, you will need to drive traffic to the page. At a minimum, you should be listing the page in all of the books you sell. If you have a page that is about a topic others are interested in, some of these people will find your page in the Facebook search engine. If you already use one or more social media platforms, you will have a better idea how you can integrate them into your publishing company.

YouTube Videos

I didn't mention YouTube on the subject of social media because I don't consider it to be in that category. YouTube has grown so big that it has become an alternative to television. The great thing about it is that it doesn't cost much, if anything, to record a video and upload it.

I know that everyone these days seems to want to be a YouTube star, but your interest should be in promoting your books. Also, keep in mind that you are not attempting to make money with your YouTube videos by monetizing them. But at the same time, if they become popular enough, it is possible to make a few dollars. What you are looking to do is get people to buy your books. Many subjects do not lend themselves to videos, but in the area of non-fiction, there are many possibilities. One example is with cooking. If you are selling cookbooks, you can demonstrate your cooking techniques and certain recipes that relate to your books or may even be contained in your book.

You don't need an expensive camera. You can use your smartphone. You don't need any fancy software either. You can transfer your file to a laptop or a desktop, and using any number of free software programs, you can edit the files. Don't worry about getting the videos perfect. In fact, don't worry about anything. The first few videos you do will only be practice runs, and you may not want to upload them to your channel.

Your voice and what you look like are unimportant. What is important is the content of the videos. Regardless of what you make your videos about, they should tie into your books. Make sure that the titles of the videos are something that people may find when doing a search on YouTube. Make sure you ask people to hit Like and Subscribe at the end of your video. Be patient. It will take time to build up an audience. But you need to tie in your videos to your books. Make sure you have links in the description of the videos and mentioned them in the videos too. You should also tie in your books to your website or blog and social media sites.

Be consistent with creating new videos, uploading, for example, once a week. In the beginning, you won't have many views, but be patient. The more videos you have, the more people will begin to find your videos. And once they find one video, they will be able to find them all.

Amazon Will Promote Your Books for Free

As amazing as this may seem, it is actually true. Amazon sends out emails to their customers all the time, promoting books they believe their customers are interested in. Much of this is related to what a person viewed recently on Amazon. However, the more your book sells, the more Amazon will promote it. This latter factor is very important. There are various ways your book will become more visible with greater sales. At the top of the list is high placement in search results, and on Amazon, good sales will lead to even more sales.

For me, this entire process begins the moment I can kick start a book with a few quick sales, then keep up the pressure for more sales. At some point the book will take on a life of its own. Of course, this is easier said than done, and for most books, it never happens. But when it does, it's a great feeling to have a book with skyrocketing sales and lucrative as well.

For the most part, you should reach for the goal of steady sales. This is not likely to happen with a non-fiction, seasonal book. In this case, you will need to ramp up your promotions at certain times of the year.

The Most Important Skill to Have with Book Promotion

Patience. Keep in mind that there are millions of books in the Amazon catalog. The number continues to climb daily, and Amazon is the number one destination for book buyers online or offline. It takes time to get people to find your books, let alone get them to buy a copy.

But make no mistake, this work must be done. As a self-publisher, you need to spend as much time promoting your books as you do writing them. If you intend to be successful, you must accept this as a part of the business. In the beginning, it is best to start with a low budget, and find your audience. Most businesses are built slowly, and writing is a business, so be patient and work hard.

I wish promotion was easy, but I'm not going to lie to you. It's a lot of hard work without any guarantee of success. It would be great if all you had to do was spend 50 dollars and get a nice return of 70 dollars: a nice recipe for success – wash, rinse, repeat. But the real world of business doesn't work that way.

If you have come this far, I want you to know that the road to success is difficult. It is part writing and part promotion, but there is no recipe for success. Even hard work is no guarantee for success, but it is a requirement. So work hard, but keep your expenses for promotion low. Be patient and give yourself and your writing time to succeed.

About The Author

I am a writer and an indie publisher who lives in Las Vegas, Nevada. My writing focuses on subjects of interest to those visiting or planning a visit to Las Vegas, Nevada. I like to write about things to do on the Strip, Downtown Las Vegas and all throughout, what we natives here call, "The Valley". I write about things to see and do, especially things off the beaten path. My goal is to help give visitors a more enjoyable experience when visiting my home town of Las Vegas.

Other Publications from Teela Books

The Big Book of Things to Do on the Las Vegas Strip by Matt Lashley
Every attraction on the Strip is listed, including sections on eating and ways to travel up and down the Strip.

Free Things To Do on the Las Vegas Strip A Self-Guided Tour by Matt Lashley
This book is a self-guided tour, taking you step by step down the Strip to visit all of the notable free things to see and do.

The Ultimate Guide to Free Things To Do in Las Vegas by Matt Lashley
This book is the ultimate guide to experiencing everything that Las Vegas has to offer that will cost you nothing.

22 Things to Do on the Las Vegas Strip for $25 and Under by Matt Lashley
The Las Vegas Strip is expensive! This books shows you all of the best tings to do for under $25.

How to Eat on the Las Vegas Strip for $10 or Less by Matt Lashley
Las Vegas doesn't want you to eat for under $10, but I have made it my mission to go up and down the Strip looking for the few possibilities that still exist.

Things To Do In Downtown Las Vegas by Matt Lashley
Read this book, and begin planning your next trip to Vegas to include Downtown Las Vegas.

Things To Do in Las Vegas Off the Strip – Away from the Neon Lights by Matt Lashley

Most of these places are not too far from the Strip and can be easily reached by car.

Shopping in Las Vegas by Matt Lashley

Learn where the best places to shop are when visiting Las Vegas.

The Best Free Photo Ops on the Las Vegas Strip by Matt Lashley

This book describes and shows photos of all of the best places to see and take pictures of, and all of these photo opportunities cost you nothing.

19 Valuable Horse Racing Betting Systems by Ken Osterman

These are methods and angles that have been among Ken Osterman's favorites over the years.

Valuable Systems, Angles and Spot Plays to Beat the Quarter Horse Races by Ken Osterman

Inside this book are a variety of approaches to quarter horse handicapping systems, angles and spot plays that are both clever and innovative.

14 Easy-To-Understand Harness Racing Betting Angles by Ken Osterman

Learn how to compute several rating methods, along with easy spot play angles.

Betting Systems for all Major Sports by Ken Osterman

This book contains systems and angles for all four of the major sports in the United States. Professional football, basketball, hockey and baseball are all covered.

The Best Sports and Horse Racing Betting Systems That Work! by Ken Osterman

This book contains the best sports and horse racing betting systems from Ken Osterman previously published in two separate books: *Sports and Horse Racing Betting Systems That Work!* and *More Sports and Horse Racing Betting Systems That Work!*

The Quick and Dirty NFL Football Handicapping Method By Ken Osterman

This method will help you find an overlay in the point spread using the simplest and quickest method possible.

How to Handicap NFL Football The Smart Way by Ken Osterman

This book contains the entire book *The Quick and Dirty NFL Football Handicapping Method*. It also contains supplemental information to improve your handicapping, along with several spot play angles.

How I Made a 13.2% Profit Betting the 2018 College Football Season with a Simple Method by Ken Osterman

This is a powerful, mechanical method for handicapping college football games.

Betting on Major League Baseball
The Underdog Method By Ken Osterman

An easy-to-understand method that creates a money line that is used to decide if an underdog is a good wager.

Sports and Horse Racing Betting Systems That Work! by Ken Osterman

The book contains some of the best sports betting systems from Ken Osterman.

More Sports and Horse Racing Betting Systems That

Work! By Ken Osterman

This is a sequel to Ken Osterman's *Sports and Horse Racing Betting Systems That Work!*. As with Ken's first book, there are methods for handicapping both horse races and sports.

The Path to Harness Racing Handicapping Profits by Douglas Masters

This book represents three decades of handicapping and betting harness races and is a summary of observations that are important to being a winning player.

Pure Speed Handicapping Quarter Horse Racing by Douglas Masters

Masters explains exactly how to create accurate speed ratings to give you an advantage over the rest of the betting public.

How to Handicap Quarter Horse Racing by Anthony T. Richards

Out of print for over 30 years, this fascinating book on handicapping quarter horse racing is now available again.

Stealth Betting Systems for Winning at Casinos by Luke Meadows

Author and casino gambler, Luke Meadows, explains his betting methods he uses in Las Vegas casinos in an easy-to-understand way.

Type 2 Diabetes: From diagnosis to a new way of life by Matthew Lashley

This book tells the story of how my diabetic condition was discovered, my denial of the condition, then the work done to get my glucose level to levels that are close to normal.

The Dream is Gone Economic Survival in 21st Century America Say No to Credit – Say No to Banks by Ron Charleston

Economic survival means breaking free from a system that takes from you and offers nothing in return. The only solution is to break free from it.

Make Money Online Without Spending Any Money by Ron Charleston
Teaches you to make money on the internet at home, from your computer, without spending a dime.

Free and Low Cost Online Promotional Techniques for Self-publishers of Kindle and POD Paperbacks by Matt Lashley
This book will teach you all of the best free and low-cost promotional techniques for your books.

The Grim Truth About Bitcoin
by Ron Charleston
This book cuts through all of the propaganda that is espoused and promulgated by the devotees of that which is called Bitcoin.

Memoirs of a Life of Confusion
by Matt Lashley
A light read about events that have confused me in childhood, family meals, school, religion, reality, language, parenting, and as an adult. I hope it will bring a smile to your face.

For the latest information about our publications, along with articles by some of our authors, please visit our website.

http://www.teela-books.com

Matt Lashley's YouTube channel *Stuck in Vegas*

Teela Books Publishing YouTube channel *Teela Books*